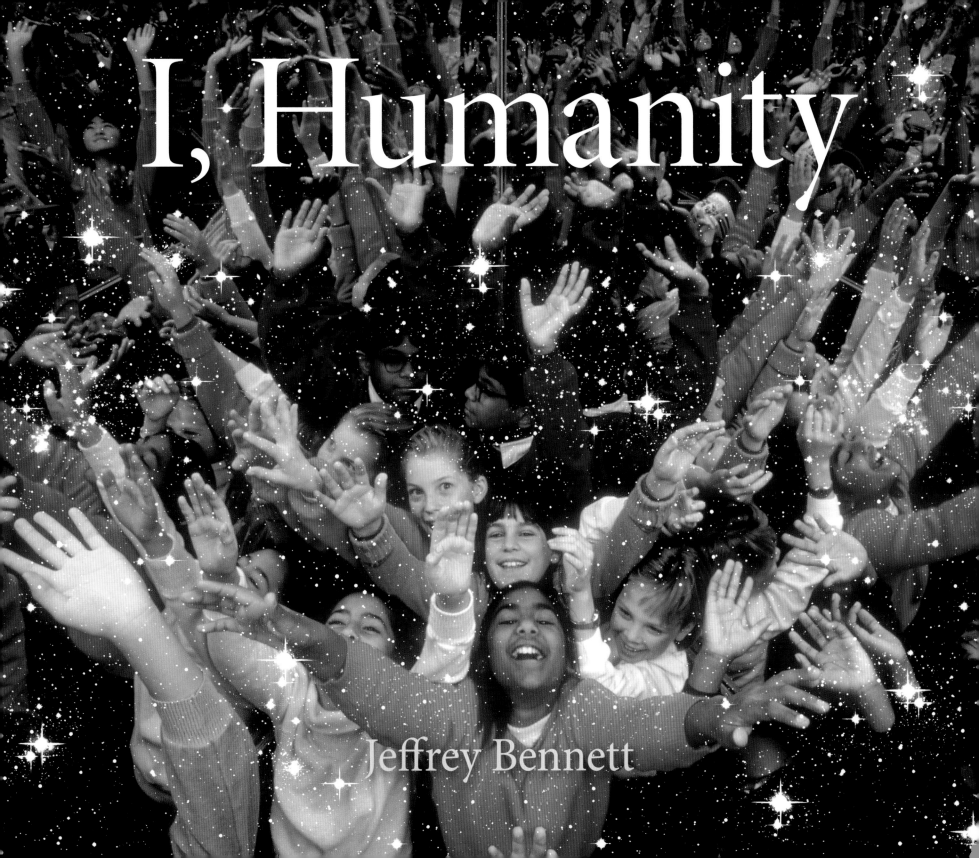

I, Humanity

Jeffrey Bennett

Design and Production: Mark Stuart Ong, Side By Side
    Studios
Editing: Joan Marsh

Published in the United States by
Big Kid Science
Boulder, Colorado
www.BigKidScience.com

ISBN: 978-1-937548-52-0
Also available in Spanish.

Illustration Credits
Cover: Phil Schermeister/Corbis
p. 3: Composite image of Earth: NASA
p. 5: Earth, solar system, universe: Pearson
p. 5: Milky Way: Mike Carroll
p. 6: The "Flammarion engraving": artist unknown;
    colorized by Roberta Weir, Garcia Weir Gallery
p. 7: Stonehenge: Wikimedia Commons/Public
    domain/ Mavratti
p. 7: Petra: Wikimedia Commons/Berthold Werner
p. 7: Angkor Wat: Wikimedia Commons/Public
    domain
p. 7: Moon images: Wikimedia Commons/Jay Tanner
p. 8: Star trails photo: Jerry Lodriguss
p. 9: Lunar eclipse photo: Itahisa González Álvarez
p. 10: Planets in sky photo: Jerry Lodriguss
p. 10: Mars retrograde photo: Cenk E. Tezel & Tunç
    Tezel
p. 12: Astrolabe: Museum of the History of Science
p. 12: Paris at night: Serge Brunier
p. 14: Galileo and telescope views: Mike Carroll
p. 15: Book: Wikimedia Commons/Andrew Dunn
p. 15: Colliding galaxies: NASA/Hubble Space
    Telescope
p. 17: Earth: NASA/ISS Expedition Crew 7
p. 18: Milky Way (both): Mike Carroll
p. 19: Hubble HXDF: NASA/Hubble Space Telescope
p. 20: Orion Nebula, Crab Nebula: NASA/Hubble
    Space Telescope

p. 21: Hubble Space Telescope and Earth: NASA/
    Hubble Space Telescope
p. 22: ISS: NASA
p. 22: Aldrin on Moon: NASA/Apollo 11
p. 22: Voyager: NASA/JPL
p. 23: Mars: NASA/JPL
p. 23: Europa: Mike Carroll
p. 23: Titan: Kees Veenenbos
p. 24: Abell 383: NASA/Hubble Space Telescope
p. 25: Both paintings: Mike Carroll
p. 26-27: Florin Prunoiu/Corbis
p. 32: Photos: NASA/JAXA

Diagrams on p. 6, 8, 9, 11, 13, 16, 17, 18, 19, 21, 24:
Adapted from Bennett, Jeffrey; Donahue, Megan;
Schneider, Nicholas; Voit, Mark, *The Cosmic
Perspective*, 7th Edition (2015), with permission of
Pearson Education, Upper Saddle River, NJ

Also by Jeffrey Bennett
For children:
    Max Goes to the Moon
    Max Goes to Mars
    Max Goes to Jupiter
    Max Goes to the Space Station
    The Wizard Who Saved the World
For grownups:
    What is Relativity?
    Math for Life
    On Teaching Science
    Beyond UFOs
Textbooks:
    The Cosmic Perspective series
    Life in the Universe
    Using and Understanding Mathematics
    Statistical Reasoning for Everyday Life

Expert Reviewers
Tomita Akihiko, Wakayama University, Japan
Georgia Bracey, Southern Illinois University
Tyson Brown, National Science Teachers Association
Megan Donahue, Michigan State University
Rosa Doran, NUCLIO, Portugal
Alvin Drew, NASA astronaut
Edward Gomez, Las Cumbres Observatory, UK
Itahisa González Álvarez, physicist, Spain
Nicole Gugliucci, Saint Anselm College
Hans Haubold, United Nations Office for Outer Space
    Affairs
Robert Hollow, CSIRO, Australia
Brian Kruse, Astronomical Society of the Pacific
Larry Lebofsky, Planetary Science Institute
Susan Lederer, NASA Johnson Space Center
Mark Levy, St. Johns University
Jim McConnell, University of Texas, Dallas
Kevin McLin, Sonoma State University
Gladys Salm, Hammer Montessori, San Jose, CA
Cecilia Scorza, Haus der Astronomie, Germany
Steve Sherman, Living Maths, South Africa
Seth Shostak, SETI Institute
Linda Strubbe, University of British Columbia
Patricia Tribe, Story Time From Space
Helen Zentner, educational consultant

Dedication

From space, we see Earth as it really is — a small and beautiful planet that we all share. I therefore dedicate this book to all members of the human race, in hopes that knowing what we have in common will inspire us to build a future of peace and prosperity that will one day enable our descendants to set sail for the stars.

I also dedicate this book to Patricia Tribe, Alvin Drew, and the astronauts of the International Space Station. Through your creation of Story Time From Space, you have once again proven that it really is possible to turn imagination into reality.

Preface

What is our place in the universe? This fundamental question has been asked by almost every person who has ever lived, but until quite recently in human history, no one really knew the answer. Today we do. Thanks to the combined efforts of scholars and scientists both male and female, and of virtually every race, religion, culture, and nationality, we now know that we live on a planet called Earth, which orbits one star (the Sun), in one galaxy (the Milky Way), in a universe filled with wonders far beyond anything our ancestors could ever have imagined.

The story of how we have learned so much about our place in the universe should fill every human with pride — and with hope for the future. After all, if we can figure out the answer to such a deep and ancient question about our existence, solving the problems of our time should be well within our capabilities.

Of course, we can only draw lessons from a story if we are familiar with it, and the sad truth is that even though this particular story belongs to the entire human race, many people have not yet had the privilege of hearing it. This book is my attempt to share the story more broadly, and hopefully in a simple and compelling way.

Please note that in keeping this book short, I've simplified many concepts, and have left out many important historical events and discoveries. I hope that readers will fill in some of these missing pieces for themselves. In addition, with help from my friends at Story Time From Space, we have created a web site that will provide you with additional details and activities you can try at home or in school; I hope you will visit it: **www.BigKidScience.com/ihumanity**.

Perhaps I am naïve, but I believe the story told here is an important one, and one that will help us all learn to work together to build a better future for all. I hope you will agree.

Reach for the stars!

Jeffrey Bennett

How to Read This Book

The main story is in the largest print.

Illustrations and their descriptions provide additional details about ideas in the story.

The narrator ("I") represents the entire human race. As you read, imagine yourself as humanity growing from childhood (long ago) to young adulthood (today).

Imagine that you could represent the entire human race, living through thousands of years of history and science. The following pages contain the story you would tell about how we've learned Earth's place in a vast universe.

▼ Our place in the universe as we know it today: Earth is a *planet* (the third from the Sun) in our *solar system*. Our solar system one of more than 100 billion star systems in the Milky Way Galaxy. Our galaxy is one of more than 100 billion galaxies in our universe.

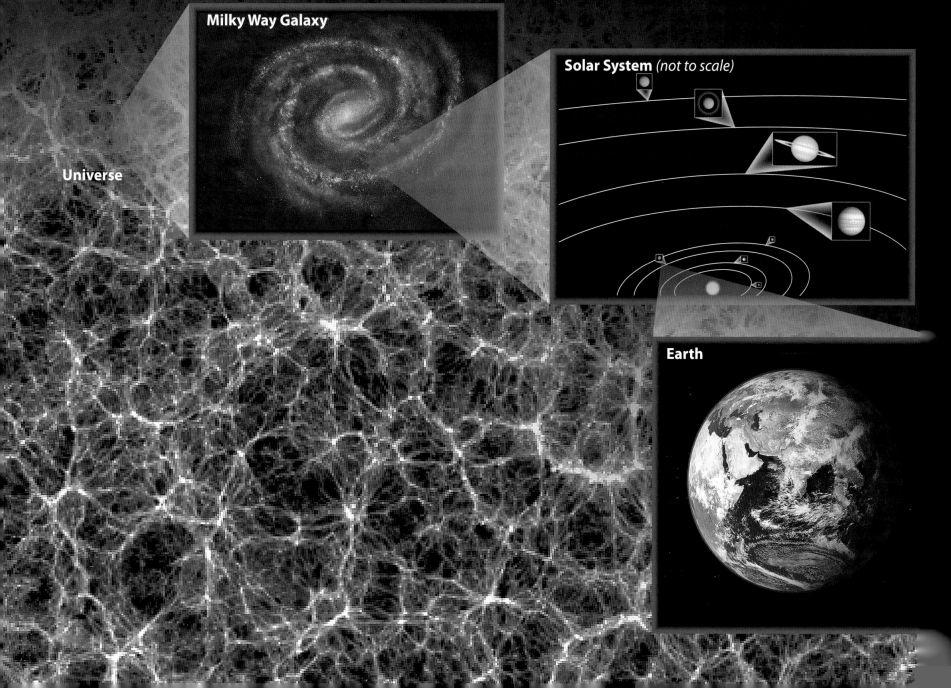

Milky Way Galaxy

Universe

Solar System (*not to scale*)

Earth

Thousands of years ago, when I was a small child, I began to try to make sense of the world around me. One of my earliest memories was seeing the star-filled sky at night, resting like a dome upon what appeared to be a flat Earth. Naturally, I thought this vision represented reality, and wondered what the Earth itself might rest upon, and what might lie beyond the stars.

Sun's path on June solstice

Sun's path on equinoxes

Sun's path on December solstice

▲ The idea of a flat Earth covered by a dome-shaped sky was common among ancient people, because it seems to explain what we see in our daily lives. After all, if you ignore hills and valleys, the Earth seems flat as you look toward the horizon, and at night the stars seem to fill a great dome extending down to the horizon in all directions.

◄ The Sun always rises in the east and sets in the west, but its precise path varies with the seasons. This diagram shows Sun paths on special dates for latitude 40°N, which includes the cities of Denver, New York, Madrid, Istanbul, Baku, and Beijing. The Sun's path changes with the seasons in a similar way at other latitudes, but with differing angles relative to the horizon (and tilting toward the north for locations in the Southern Hemisphere).

As centuries passed, I began to recognize patterns of motion in the sky. I learned to tell time by the Sun, and to keep track of the seasons by observing changes in the Sun's precise daily path. I observed how the Moon changes shape in a cycle of phases that repeats every 29 to 30 days. Near the sea, I saw the tides changing with these phases. At night, I learned to navigate by the stars, and saw how the visible constellations change along with the seasons.

Sunday	Monday	Tuesday	Wednesday	Thursday	Friday	Saturday
				1	2	3
4	5	6	7	8	9	10
11	12	13	14	15	16	17
18	19	20	21	22	23	24
25	26	27	28	29	30	

▲ Many ancient people built structures to help them observe the Sun's changing path, so that they could keep track of the seasons for agriculture, hunting, and religious practices.

▲ The Moon's cycle of phases (shown as they appear in the Northern Hemisphere) repeats about every 29½ days; the length of the month (think "moonth") is based on this cycle. Tides change with the Moon's phases, because tides are caused by the gravity of the Sun and Moon. Tides are strongest at new and full moons, when the Sun and Moon pull the tides along the same line, and weaker in between, when the pulls of the Sun and Moon are in different directions.

I began using my navigation skills to travel. To my surprise, I discovered new constellations as I journeyed north or south. Clearly, there was more to Earth and sky than I saw from home. With this knowledge, I soon understood what I saw during *lunar eclipses*, when Earth's shadow falls on the Moon. The shadow's gentle curvature could only mean that our world is round.

In place of my old idea of a flat Earth with a domed sky, I began to imagine the sky as a great sphere containing the Sun, Moon, and stars, with our round Earth located at its center.

▼ Stars follow circular paths over the course of the night, centered on a point that depends on your location (latitude). As you move north or south, that central point moves higher or lower in your sky, proving that there is more to the sky than what you can see from any one place.

north celestial pole

Milky Way   Cassiopeia   Perseus
Andromeda
Aries
Pegasus
Pisces   Taurus
ecliptic (Sun's path)
celestial equator
Aquarius
Eridanus
Cetus
Fornax
Sculptor
Phoenix

south celestial pole

◄ This diagram shows the ancient idea of Earth at the center of a great *celestial sphere*. In reality, every star lies at a different distance from Earth; the stars appear to lie on a celestial sphere because they are so far away that our eyes cannot notice their differing distances. The Sun and Moon also appear to lie on this sphere, with the Sun moving around it once each year and the Moon moving around it about once each month.

My new idea seemed to make a lot of sense. I could explain the daily paths of the Sun, Moon, and stars in my sky by picturing the great sphere spinning once each day around our Earth. To account for the changing seasons and the phases of the Moon, I imagined the Sun and Moon moving slowly among the constellations on the giant sphere.

▼ From any particular location, you can typically see a lunar eclipse once every year or two. Here, from left to right, we see several images taken during the first hour of an eclipse, as Earth's shadow moves across the Moon's face. The roundness of the shadow demonstrates that Earth is a sphere.

◄ The celestial sphere appears to turn around us once each day, which is why stars all seem to circle around a central point in the sky; notice that this point is directly above either Earth's north or south pole, depending on where you live. Today, we know that it is *Earth* that rotates each day, not the sky. Earth rotates from west to east, which is why the Sun, Moon, planets, and stars (those whose daily circles take them below the horizon) appear to rise in the east and set in the west.

Still, there was one thing that puzzled me. My eyes could see five bright "stars" that, like the Sun and Moon, did not stay fixed in the constellations. But instead of moving steadily in one direction like the Sun and Moon, these five objects sometimes turned around and went backward for a few weeks or months. I called them *planets,* and for a while I wondered if they had minds of their own.

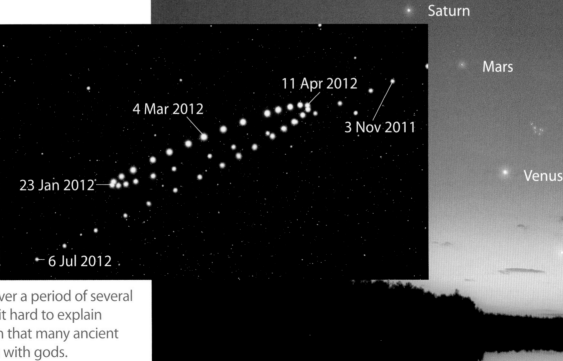

▼ Only five of the planets we know today shine brightly enough to have been recognized in ancient times. This photo shows them together in the sky in 2002; they won't appear so close together again until 2040. Interestingly, because the word *planet* (Greek for "wanderer") originally referred to objects that appear to move among the stars in our sky, in ancient times the "planets" included the Sun and Moon but not Earth. That made a total of 7 "planets," which is how the calendar ended up with 7 days in a week.

▶ On any single night, each planet rises in the east and sets in the west. But if you watch over many nights, you'll see that the planets move gradually among the stars. And unlike the Sun and Moon, which always move in the same direction through the constellations, planets follow paths in which they sometimes seem to turn around and go backward. This image combines photos of Mars in the night sky taken over a period of several months. Ancient people found it hard to explain this motion, which is one reason that many ancient mythologies associated planets with gods.

I spent centuries trying to understand the mysterious patterns of the planets. Finally, about 2,000 years ago, I hit upon an idea that seemed to work — at least for a while.

I imagined that each planet orbited around Earth on a small circle that turned upon a larger one, so that the planet would go backward when on the inner part of its circle. I used mathematics to make my picture of circles upon circles more precise, so that I could use it to predict when and where the planets would appear in the night sky.

planet

Earth

▲ To explain the fact that the Sun, Moon, and planets move among the stars, scholars of ancient Greece proposed that each of these objects moved on its own sphere, each nested within an outer sphere of stars. This allowed them to explain the motion of the Sun and Moon by assuming that these two spheres turned slightly slower than the sphere of the stars. But it still did not explain the strange motions of the planets.

▶ Beginning about 2,200 years ago, Greek scholars came up with an idea that seemed to work: They imagined each planet turning on a small circle, while the small circle went around a larger circle with Earth at the center. The diagram shows how this would make a planet appear to go backward — just as we see for Mars on the left-hand page — when it is on the inner part of the small circle. This Earth-centered model — meaning a scientific idea that seems to explain something and can be used to make predictions — was put in mathematical form by Claudius Ptolemy in about A.D. 150.

For more than a thousand years, I thought I had it all figured out. Earth was the center of the universe, the stars lay on a great sphere surrounding us, and the planets moved along their circles upon circles. But as time passed and I built better tools for measurement, my predictions about planet locations in the night sky no longer seemed to work well. I began to question everything I thought I knew. Could all my ideas about the universe be wrong?

▼ Ptolemy's Earth-centered model with circles upon circles remained in use for more than 1,400 years, in part because it worked fairly well. But as time passed, errors became more noticeable. Near its far left, this photo of Paris at night shows Jupiter about 3 degrees (out of 360 degrees in a circle) from the Moon. By the time of the European Renaissance, Ptolemy's model often made predictions that, for example, put Jupiter on the wrong side of the Moon.

▶ Better tools for measurement made the flaws of Ptolemy's model more obvious. This photo shows one such tool, called an astrolabe. Like many other tools of science, the astrolabe was greatly improved by scholars working at the world's first true university: the "House of Wisdom" in Baghdad. There, the Islamic scholars who built it worked closely with scholars of many other religions and cultures.

One day, I tried a new idea. Instead of imagining everything going around Earth, I envisioned Earth and the other planets orbiting the Sun. I had long realized that this idea could explain the puzzling motion of planets, because a planet would seem to move backward whenever we passed it by in our orbit. I hadn't taken this idea very seriously in the past, but now I worked hard to test whether it might really be true.

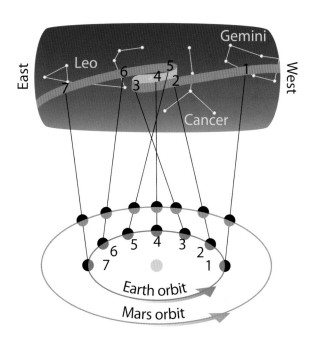

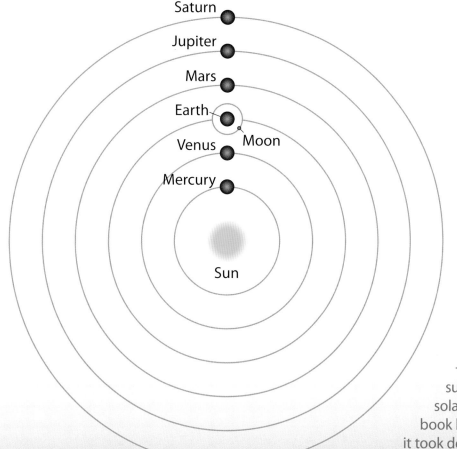

▲ This diagram shows how the Sun-centered model simply explains the seemingly strange motion of Mars. Both Earth and Mars always orbit in the same direction around the Sun, but Earth orbits faster. By connecting the dots at their different orbital positions, you can see that this causes Mars to *appear* to turn around and go backward (relative to the stars) as we pass it by.

◄ In 1543, Nicolas Copernicus published a book in which he suggested that the Sun, rather than Earth, is the center of our solar system. He was not the first person to have this idea, but his book brought it much more attention than ever before. Although it took decades for other scientists to work out the details, we now know that his basic idea was correct: Earth and the other planets really do orbit the Sun, and the stars are much farther away.

I soon discovered laws with which I could predict the locations of planets so precisely that I was almost sure my new idea was correct. I became even more convinced after I built my first telescopes. I saw moons orbiting Jupiter, proving that Earth was not the center of everything. I saw Venus appearing to change shape in a way that proved it orbited the Sun and not Earth. And I saw that the *Milky Way* stretching across my sky is made up of countless stars, which was proof that there is much more to the universe than meets the eye. By about 400 years ago, there was no more doubt in my mind: Earth is *not* the center of the universe, but just one of the planets orbiting our Sun.

▼ Beginning in 1609, Galileo built telescopes that he used to look at the night sky. Here, we see him with three early discoveries that helped prove that Earth really does orbit the Sun.

Stars in the Milky Way

Venus phases

Jupiter's moons

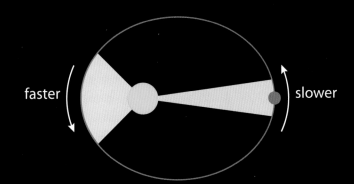

faster   slower

▲ Copernicus assumed that planets would have perfect-circle orbits around the Sun, but they don't. The true shape of planet orbits was discovered by Johannes Kepler. The diagram shows Kepler's first two laws of planetary motion, published in 1609: (1) Each planet's orbit has the shape of an *ellipse*, with the Sun slightly off-center (at a *focus*); and (2) a planet moves faster in the part of its orbit when it is closer to the Sun (the two triangles show the more technical statement of this law—that a planet always sweeps out an equal area in equal amounts of time). Kepler's laws give virtually perfect predictions of planet positions in the sky.

Now that I knew the planets orbited the Sun, I began to wonder *why*. To find out, I used the same approach that had worked so well for me already. I made careful observations, I looked for simple ways of making sense of these observations, and I used mathematics to make predictions that I could test with more observations. I called this approach *science*, and it soon provided my answer: The very same gravity that keeps my feet on the ground also holds the Moon in orbit around the Earth and the planets in orbit around the Sun. I had discovered that I live in a *uni*verse, in which the same laws hold both on Earth and in space.

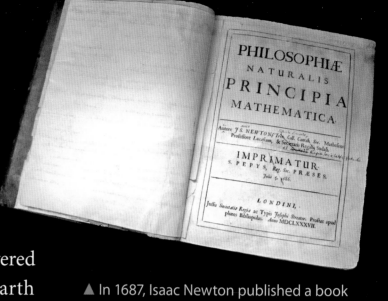

▲ In 1687, Isaac Newton published a book that included his discovery of the law of gravity. He said his moment of insight came when he saw an apple fall and realized that the same gravity that causes its fall also holds the Moon in orbit around Earth, and the planets in orbit around the Sun.

◀ Gravity works the same way everywhere in the universe, always attracting one object to others. It attracts us to Earth, which is why we stay on the ground. It attracts the planets to the Sun, and this fact combined with their motion explains why the planets orbit the Sun. Gravity even attracts distant galaxies to one another, sometimes leading them to collide.

15

My new way of doing science also helped me create new technologies. Soon, I was building more and larger telescopes, and each new telescope led me to new discoveries. I saw the ice caps of Mars and the rings of Saturn. I discovered two new planets that I'd never noticed with my eyes alone. I also found many smaller objects orbiting the Sun along with the planets. At last, I realized that our Earth is just one member of a vast family of worlds held together by the Sun's gravity. I call this family our *solar system*.

▼ Our solar system as we know it today. The four inner planets are relatively small and close together. The four outer planets are much larger and farther apart. *Asteroids* are smaller than planets and are made of rock and metal; most of them are found in the *asteroid belt* between the orbits of Mars and Jupiter. *Comets* are similar to asteroids except they contain a lot of ice; most orbit far beyond the planets. Some of the largest asteroids and comets, such as Ceres, Pluto, and Eris, are often called "dwarf planets." (This diagram magnifies the planets about a thousand times relative to their orbits, and the Sun is *not* shown on the same scale; the Sun is about 10 times as large in diameter as Jupiter, so it would fill the page on the scale used here for the planets.)

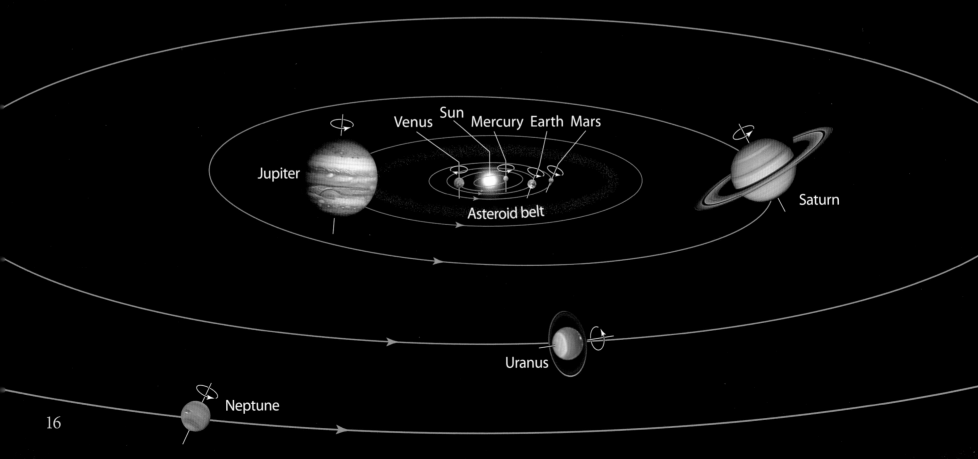

Most astonishingly, I came to realize that the stars are not mere lights in the night sky. The stars are distant suns, and each would appear as big and bright to a planet orbiting one of them as our Sun does to us. I wondered if any of the stars really did have planets of their own, and if so, whether those planets might have beings who see our Sun as a star in their night sky.

distant stars

nearby star

July

January

▲ Today, astronomers can measure distances to many stars very precisely. To understand how, extend your hand and hold your finger still, then alternately open and close your left and right eyes. Notice that even though your finger is still, it *appears* to shift back and forth. In the same way, the position of a star shifts slightly as we view it at different times of year. The amount of the shift, or *parallax*, allows us to calculate the star's distance.

▼ By the late 1600s, scientists began to realize that the Sun is a star, and that the stars we see at night are dim only because they are so far away. Christiaan Huygens, whose quotation you see below, was one of the first to recognize this fact and to understand the true size of our solar system.

"How vast those Orbs must be, and how inconsiderable this Earth, the Theatre upon which all our mighty Designs, all our Navigations, and all our Wars are transacted, is when compared to them. A very fit consideration, and matter of Reflection, for those Kings and Princes who sacrifice the Lives of so many People, only to flatter their Ambition in being Masters of some pitiful corner of this small Spot." — Christiaan Huygens, 1690

I was rapidly learning that the universe is far larger than I ever dreamed in my youth. As I studied the arrangement of stars in the sky, I discovered that our Sun is part of a great collection of stars that I now call the *Milky Way Galaxy*. The galaxy has so many stars — more than 100 billion — that it would take me thousands of years just to count them out loud! We live fairly far from the center of the galaxy, and our solar system orbits around the center about once every 200 million years.

You are here

▲ This painting shows our Milky Way Galaxy as it might appear if we could see it from the outside. The bright disk, with its central bulge and spiral arms, shines with the combined light of more than 100 billion stars, along with great clouds of gas and dust from which new stars will be born. The arrow indicates the approximate location of our solar system, which is about halfway out through the disk.

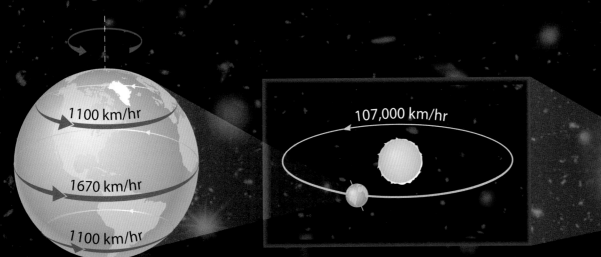

1100 km/hr

1670 km/hr

1100 km/hr

107,000 km/hr

800,000 km/hr

▲ We may feel like we are "sitting still" on Earth, but we are actually on a high-speed journey. Earth's daily rotation carries most of us around (the rotation axis) at more than 1000 kilometers per hour. We travel at more than 100,000 kilometers per hour in our yearly orbit around the Sun. And along with our entire solar system, we orbit around the galaxy's center at a speed of about 800,000 kilometers per hour.

The biggest change in my perspective was still to come. For a while, I was unsure if anything lay beyond the bounds of our Milky Way. But as I built even larger telescopes, I realized that the universe is full of galaxies, some so far away that their light has taken billions of years to reach us. I also discovered that the galaxies are moving farther apart with time. Apparently, our entire universe is expanding, meaning that it was smaller in the past and will grow larger in the future.

▲ In 1929, Edwin Hubble (for whom the Hubble Space Telescope was named) announced his discovery that galaxies throughout the universe are moving farther apart with time. In other words, the entire universe is getting larger, or *expanding*, as time passes. The three cubes show the idea for a small portion of the universe. The cube at the left represents the distant past, when galaxies were much closer together, and the cube on the right represents the galaxies as they are today.

▲ Today we know that our universe is filled with galaxies, each containing millions or billions of stars — and most of those stars probably have planets that orbit around them. Because it takes light time to cross the vast distances in space, we see distant galaxies as they were long in the past, when the light we see began its journey. Some of the galaxies in this photo from the Hubble Space Telescope are so far away that their light has taken 12 billion years to reach us.

Over the past century, my knowledge has grown at an ever-faster rate. I've discovered much more about the laws of nature that govern everything from tiny atoms to groups of galaxies. I've used these laws to figure out how stars and planets are born, and how stars live and die. My understanding of the laws of nature has also helped me recognize that the universe contains some very strange objects, including *black holes*, which actually bend space and time.

▼ The Orion Nebula is a great cloud of gas and dust in which we can see new stars and planets being born.

▲ The Crab Nebula is the remains of a star that ended its life in the type of titanic explosion called a *supernova*.

▼ This computer simulation shows what you might see if you looked toward a black hole with stars visible behind it. Notice the strange arcs of light, and double images of stars, caused by the way the black hole distorts space and time. These distortions are explained by Einstein's *theory of relativity*.

I've built larger and larger telescopes, and have launched some telescopes into space, where they enable me to see forms of light that cannot pass through the air to reach the ground. Using computers to help analyze all the data, I've begun to understand the size and age of our entire universe. I've also confirmed that other stars really do have their own planets, and that many of these planets have sizes and orbits very similar to those of Earth.

Dozens of telescopes have been launched into space, including the Hubble Space Telescope, shown here as it orbits above Earth.

▶ All the colors that our eyes can see make up what we call *visible light*. There are many other forms of light that our eyes cannot see. This diagram lists different forms of light and shows how far they penetrate from space into our atmosphere. Notice that much of this light does not reach the ground, and therefore can only be studied with telescopes at high altitudes or in space.

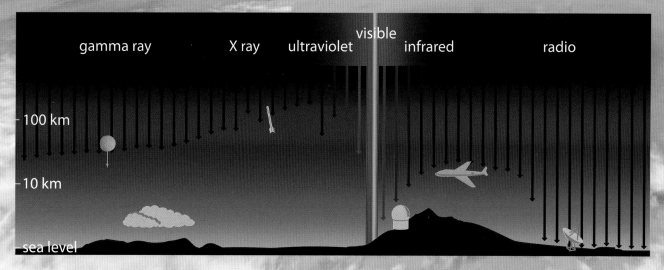

| gamma ray | | X ray | ultraviolet | visible | infrared | radio |

100 km

10 km

sea level

21

I've even begun to travel out into space myself. I have built space stations from which I can observe Earth from orbit. I've walked on the Moon. And while I have yet to go elsewhere myself, I've sent robot spacecraft throughout our solar system.

▼ The International Space Station orbits Earth every 90 minutes. Since its construction, it has been visited by more than 200 astronauts representing more than a dozen nations and numerous cultures and religions.

▲ The first human visit to another world occurred in July, 1969, when astronauts Neil Armstrong and Buzz Aldrin landed on the Moon. Humans have not yet visited any other world.

▲ We've sent robot spacecraft to all the planets and many moons, asteroids, and comets. This painting shows *Voyager 2*, which visited the planets Jupiter, Saturn, Uranus, and Neptune and continues its outward journey today.

These robots make me yearn for my own trips. Soon, I hope, I'll explore the mountains and valleys of Mars, walk across the ice of Jupiter's moon Europa, and sail the seas of Saturn's moon Titan. I often wonder if I'll find living creatures on these or any other worlds in our Sun's family.

▲ This painting shows the surface of Jupiter's moon Europa, with Jupiter in the background. Europa is covered by a thick layer of ice, but scientists suspect that there is an ocean of salty water beneath the ice. Could there be living creatures swimming in Europa's perpetually dark ocean?

▶ Saturn's moon Titan is much too cold for liquid water, but it has rivers, lakes, and seas of extremely cold liquid methane and ethane. Here, we see a painting that imagines what we might see if we sailed on one of Titan's lakes.

▲ Mars has some of the largest mountains and deepest canyons in the solar system. Here, we see the surface of Mars photographed from the robot rover called *Curiosity*. Although Mars is dry today, robotic spacecraft have found clear evidence of past lakes and possibly seas, making scientists wonder if Mars was ever home to life.

Despite all I've learned, I still have many questions left to answer. I know what planets and stars are made of, but I've discovered that galaxies also contain a mysterious *dark matter* whose nature still eludes me. Stranger still, I've discovered that the galaxies are moving apart faster today than long ago, and while I sometimes say this is caused by *dark energy*, I really don't know what it is or why it exists.

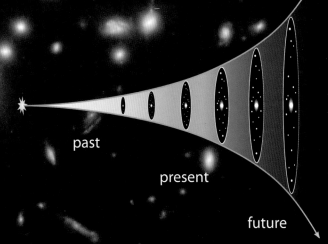

▼ Careful observations of the rate of expansion show that the universe today is expanding faster than it was in the past. Scientists say that the expansion is *accelerating* — but no one yet knows why.

past

present

future

▲ Large clusters of galaxies often appear to have big arcs of light like those shown here. These arcs are actually distorted images of other galaxies that lie behind the cluster; the cluster's gravity distorts the light in the same way that a black hole can distort light. Studying these images allows scientists to calculate the strength of gravity, and these studies reveal that most matter in the universe does not give off light, which is why it is called *dark matter*. No one yet knows what it is actually made of.

And, of course, I wonder if I am alone, or if there are others like me, living on some of the billions of planets that orbit other stars. My imagination runs wild as I think of all different types of life and civilizations that might be out there, somewhere.

▼ Scientists have recently learned that planets are common around other stars, and that many of these planets are likely to be similar in character to Earth. Here, we see two imaginary scenes of possible other worlds. The smaller painting (below) shows a planet much like Earth, with the lights of its own civilization, that orbits a double star. The larger painting (full page) shows the view from the surface of a planet orbiting a star just outside the Milky Way galaxy, so that the entire galaxy is visible in its night sky.

But for now, I bring my thoughts back down to Earth, to reflect on all I've learned. In a relatively short time, I have made an incredible scientific journey. Where once I believed myself to be the center of the universe, I now know that I am just one species, living on one small planet, orbiting one ordinary star, within just one of billions of galaxies in a vast universe.

Most important, I've come to realize that as I've learned more about my place in the universe, I've also learned more about myself. I may be physically small, but when I put my mind to it, I am capable of great things.

For I am humanity, and I am still young. If I continue to build and learn, there is no limit to what my future may hold.

Glossary

asteroids Relatively small, rocky objects that orbit the Sun.

black hole A strange type of astronomical object in which matter is compressed so much that not even light can escape. Astronomers have discovered many black holes, and they are understood through Einstein's theory of relativity.

celestial sphere The celestial sphere represents the way stars all appear to lie on a great sphere around Earth; it is an illusion created by the fact that our eyes cannot perceive the differing distances of stars.

comets Relatively small, icy objects that orbit the Sun; similar to asteroids except with more ice and usually farther from the Sun.

constellations Regions of the sky identified by visible patterns of stars.

dark energy The name given to the unknown energy or force that is apparently causing the expansion of the universe to get faster with time.

dark matter The name given to the unknown form of matter that, based on its gravitational effects, appears to represent most of the matter in the universe.

dwarf planets A name given to large, round objects — including Ceres, Pluto, and Eris — that orbit the Sun but are not quite big enough to count as official planets.

ellipse A special type of oval that happens to be the shape of all planetary orbits, as well as of the orbits of moons and other objects.

expanding universe The term we use to describe the fact that the space between galaxies is growing with time.

galaxy A great island of stars in space, containing millions, billions, or even trillions of stars, all held together by gravity and orbiting a common center.

gravity A force that attracts masses together. In general, more massive objects have stronger gravity. For example, your body has little gravity, Earth has enough gravity to hold you to the ground, and the Sun has enough gravity to keep the rest of the solar system orbiting around it.

Kepler's laws (of planetary motion) The laws that describe how planets orbit around our Sun.

latitude A measure of angular distance from the equator; the equator is latitude 0°, the north pole is latitude 90°N, and the south pole is latitude 90°S.

lunar eclipse An event that occurs when the Moon passes through Earth's shadow, which can occur only at full moon.

Milky Way Galaxy The galaxy in which we live.

model (scientific) A representation of some aspect of nature that can be used to explain and predict real phenomena.

moon An object that orbits a planet (or dwarf planet, etc.).

nebula A cloud of gas (and dust) in space.

parallax The apparent shifting of an object's position against the background, due to viewing it from different locations.

phases (such as those of the Moon or Venus) The changing appearance of an object as we see different portions of its sunlit and night sides.

planet A relatively large object that orbits a star. Our solar system has eight official planets: Mercury, Venus, Earth, Mars, Jupiter, Saturn, Uranus, and Neptune.

relativity (theory of) Our best current explanation for the nature of space, time, and gravity; first discovered by Einstein.

science The search for knowledge that can be used to explain or predict natural phenomena in a way that can be confirmed by observations or experiments.

solar system (or star system) Our solar system consists of the Sun and all the objects that orbit it, including the planets, moons, asteroids, and comets. Other stars have similar systems of orbiting objects.

star A large, glowing ball of very hot gas; our Sun is a star.

universe All the galaxies and everything within and between them, which is the same as saying the sum total of all matter and energy in existence.

Suggested Activities

Find additional activities and related resources at www.BigKidScience.com.

Cultural Astronomy (All Grade Levels)

Through research or asking your elders, find out what people of your culture believed about the universe in ancient times. Discuss with others why these beliefs would have made sense at the time, even though they may differ from our modern understanding of the universe.

Observing the Sky (Grades 3 and Up)

Our ancestors were very familiar with the sky, both day and night, but indoor life and electric lighting mean that many people no longer have this familiarity. Try to acquaint yourself with the sky with the following:

- Observe the Sun's path: Choose a location where you have a relatively clear horizon and draw sketches of the horizon to the east and west (for example, show buildings and trees). Go to your location at sunrise  and sunset, and mark the Sun's rise and set positions on your sketches. Also go out at mid-day, when the Sun is highest in your sky, and use your extended arm to measure how high the Sun is in "fists" above the horizon. Repeat every one to two weeks for several months, and observe how the Sun's path changes over this period.
- Moon phases: Make a calendar for at least one month, and each day draw a picture of what the Moon looks like in your sky. (Because the Moon is  sometimes visible only in the afternoon/ evening and sometimes only in the morning, be sure to look for the Moon both morning and evening each day.) When you finish the month, make a list of all the things you notice about the Moon's cycle of phases, and try to explain the reasons for each of those things.
- Star paths: Go outside late on a clear night, and identify at least three bright stars — one that is located toward the south, one that is high above your head,  and one that is located toward the north. Draw sketches with neighboring stars, so that you'll be able to identify the same bright stars another night. Then go out early on another night, and starting just after dark, find your stars about once every hour until bedtime. Can you figure out how the stars move across your sky?
- Planets: Use the Web to find out when Mars or Jupiter is visible in your night sky. Then, once a week for at least two months, make a sketch of where the  planet is located relative to stars around it. Is the planet moving east or west relative to the stars? Does it go through any "backward" motion during the period in which you are observing it? By referring to the illustration on page 13, try to figure out the relative positions of Earth and Mars or Jupiter in their orbits during the time of your observations.

Counting Stars (Grades 5 and Up)

In the story (page 18), it says it would take thousands of years to count the stars in the Milky Way galaxy. Let's make a more accurate estimate. Assume the galaxy has 100 billion (100,000,000,000) stars, though the actual number may be a few times higher. Also assume you can count one star each second, so that it would take you 100 billion seconds to count them all. Using simple division (calculator optional), figure out how many minutes, hours, days, and years this is. Then discuss how this fact affects your perspective on the size of our galaxy and of the universe.

Vast Orbs (Grades 5 and Up)

Let's get a sense of the relative sizes of things in our solar system. The table below shows real data for the Sun, Earth, and Jupiter. Do the following:

- We'll use a scale of 1 to 10 billion, so divide each value by 10 billion to get its scaled value. Then put the sizes in units of centimeters and the distances in units of meters. (Remember that 1 kilometer = 1000 meters and 1 meter = 100 centimeters.)
- Find something about the correct scaled size for each object (such as a ball or round fruit for the Sun, and a marble or pinhead for each planet). Put your Sun in a central location and then walk to the correct scaled distances with your Earth and Jupiter. Remember that the planets orbit the Sun at these distances, Earth taking 1 year for each orbit and Jupiter taking about 12 years.

- The Moon is a little more than ¼ the size of Earth and located about 400,000 kilometers from Earth. Where does it go on this scale?
- Write about or discuss how seeing these objects to scale affects your perspective. Does it help you understand the quotation from Huygens on page 17?

Object	Diameter	Distance from Sun
Sun	1,400,000 km	—
Earth	12,800 km	150,000,000 km
Jupiter	143,000 km	778,000,000 km

Creative Writing — *The Cosmic Perspective* (Grades 5 and up)

This book has introduced what is sometimes called the *cosmic perspective,* meaning the way that our modern understanding of the universe changes our perspective on ourselves and our planet Earth. Express your own thoughts about the cosmic perspective through creative writing, using a form of your choice (such as a short story, a play, or a poem).

Research Project (Grades 7 and Up)

Choose one topic in the book that you'd like to know more about. A few examples: the Apollo visits to the Moon, robotic missions to Mars, how stars and planets are born, black holes, the expanding universe, or dark matter or dark energy. Use the Web to learn more about your topic, and write a short paper about it.

A Note to Parents and Teachers

I, Humanity is designed to be much more than just a book. It is intended to be a part of an educational experience that will help your children or your students reach their full potential. To this end, you should be aware of key ideas that will help you make the best use of this book.

Within the book itself: Like all Big Kid Science books, *I, Humanity* incorporates what we call the three pillars of successful learning: *education, perspective,* and *inspiration.*

- The education pillar is the specific content that we want students to learn; in this book, the education pillar includes understanding how science uses observations and logical thinking to learn about the world around us.
- The perspective pillar shows students how what they are learning can affect their views on their own lives and on humanity's place in the universe.
- The inspiration pillar encourages students to want to learn more, and to think about how they personally can help make this world a better place.

When reading this book with your children or students, be sure to focus on all three pillars through activities or discussion.

The book web site: We will be posting additional resources on the book web site, including details about the concepts on each page, activities, and more. Be sure to visit the web site: **www.BigKidScience.com/ihumanity**.

Story Time From Space: *I, Humanity* is part of the exciting new Story Time From Space program, in which astronauts read books and conduct related science demos aboard the International Space Station. The videos and other education resources are then posted freely at: **www.StoryTimeFromSpace.com**.

◄ The book *The Wizard Who Saved the World* floats in front of a window on the International Space Station.

▼ Astronaut Koichi Wakata prepares to read *Max Goes to the Space Station* in Japanese.